DEEPER
MORE
MEANINGFUL
LIFE

DEEPER MORE MEANINGFUL LIFE

by Lawrence Neisent

TATE PUBLISHING
AND ENTERPRISES, LLC

Deeper More Meaningful Life
Copyright © 2014 by Lawrence Neisent. All rights reserved.

Published by Tate Publishing & Enterprises, LLC
127 E. Trade Center Terrace | Mustang, Oklahoma 73064 USA
1.888.361.9473 | www.tatepublishing.com

Tate Publishing is committed to excellence in the publishing industry. The company reflects the philosophy established by the founders, based on Psalm 68:11,
"The Lord gave the word and great was the company of those who published it."

Book design copyright © 2014 by Tate Publishing, LLC. All rights reserved.
Cover design by Rtor Maghuyop
Interior design by Jimmy Sevilleno

Published in the United States of America

ISBN: 978-1-63306-633-5
1. Self-Help / Personal Growth / General
2. Religion / Christian Life / Family
14.07.31

CONTENTS

MAKING MOMENTS INTO MEMORIES

Mundane moments are opportunities for treasured memories when carefully handled rather than carelessly wasted. Each chapter in this book has its own voice. Together, they form a chorus of ideas designed to empower the reader to actionable conclusions. Any steps toward a deeper, more meaningful life are steps in the right direction.

Right up front, I'd like to challenge you to translate the ideas and suggestions into your season or situation in life. If you don't have children, you are still called to parent young men and women as Paul fathered Timothy in the faith. If you aren't married, discover your Jonathan and David covenant relationships to invest in as treasured connections. The key in all of these ideas is to discover the amazing treasure of relationships that have been entrusted to your care in the various seasons of life. This moves us from mere life to enriched life.

An enriched and fulfilling life is easier than most people think. This is not about having the most of what we want but making the most of what we have. It's not that this is some incredibly complicated thing to do. It's simply a matter of making a priority of those things that should be prioritized.

At the core, this is not about pursuing a deeper, more meaningful life for you as much as it's about providing it for others. The more self-serving we are in our pursuit of life, the less life we will experience. May our efforts, energy, priorities, and passion be devoted to improve the lives of those we love.

If you call something a priority but you have no energy or resources devoted to it, call it something else. It's not a priority. What we believe has an effect on how we behave. The problem is that there is often a breakdown between what we believe and how we behave.

Thousands of times I've stood before groups of people asking if they believe. "Yes, we believe!" replies the crowd. Then I ask, "Will you behave?" "We will behave!" comes the common response. We all want to live better lives, but the question is, can we translate what we believe into how we behave.

Do you believe that family is important? Yes! You believe, but how do you behave? What kind of routine behavior do you have in place that legitimizes your belief? Designating a family night together each week and having a meal around the table legitimize the belief that our family is important. A weekly date night with our spouse legitimizes the belief that our marriage is a priority. Taking my daughters on daddy–daughter dates routinely legitimizes what I believe by structuring how I behave consistently. Structure substantiates what we believe by perpetuating a behavior.

Saying "I love you" is important. Carrying those words into a constantly devoted action is how you substantiate what you believe by how you behave. This isn't a rigid and legalistic requirement. It's a routine, a structure to which we devote ourselves. There are times our date night or our family night doesn't happen at home, but missing these prioritized times together aren't the rule, they're the exception.

It's amazing how much life returns to us when we purpose to invest it into the lives of others. It is more blessed to give than to receive. A deeper, more meaningful life is the reward of discovering how to more effectively care for the people God has entrusted to our lives. This book is filled with simple suggestions and easy ideas that will empower you to experience the abundant life that Jesus desires for you to experience.

My youngest daughter, Lexi, asked if I would take her for a daddy–daughter picnic sometime. Schedules were tight and she had school, but I told her I'd see what I could do. Realizing the weather wasn't conducive for a picnic, I decided to make it happen anyway. The next day, I checked her out of school fifteen minutes before her lunchtime. We quickly went to my office to stay within the one-hour time-frame we had. As we walked in, the lights were low, a blanket was spread on the floor, food was ready, and my laptop was on the desk with a waterfall playing from *YouTube*. As far as Lexi was concerned, we were in the woods!

Meaningful memories are inexpensive to create and priceless to remember.

As a young man, I learned the importance of finding mentors in prioritized areas of my life. I wanted to experience life from a more meaningful perspective. When Tracy and I were married, we sought out mentors together. As parents and now leaders in our community, we've learned the value of mentorship on entirely new levels. From these mentors, we have gained a wealth of ideas, suggestions, and illustrations that convert a house into a home, a mere job into a career, a relationship into a life-giving friendship, and a marriage into an expression of true covenant. There is life, and then there is a deeper, more meaningful life. The difference between the two is experientially vast yet requires very little effort to get there.

Are you ready to experience a deeper, more meaningful life?

EXTRAORDINARY

THE DIFFERENCE BETWEEN ordinary and *extra*ordinary is obviously just a little *extra*. It's amazing how easily an ordinary situation can be converted into an extraordinary experience. Something as ordinary as a pizza night can be converted into an extraordinary evening if the lighting is low, the music is right, and a candle is lit.

It's not merely trying to make a special moment that is the key. The real difference comes when your purpose is to make it special for somebody you care about. This makes for an extraordinary friendship, an extraordinary marriage, an extraordinary family, or for any relationship you want to make from ordinary to extraordinary.

Prov 24:3 says, "It takes wisdom to have a good family, and it takes understanding to make it strong" (NCV).

Understanding what people around you love and appreciate is important to making those relationships extraordinary. After forty years of marriage, Harriet was buttering the toast, doing what she'd done for decades when the loaf was new and when it was almost gone. She placed the heel in front of the love her life. In frustration, Carl asked, "Why do you always give me the heel?!" Harriet replied, "I'm sorry! I've always given you the heel because it's my favorite piece of the bread."

Take risks and take notes. Taking risks to express that extra effort is a nice touch to any relational effort. Taking notes and purposing to remember what is valued are what turn years of relationship into an extraordinary legacy.

Deeper, more meaningful lives are the result of these little extra considerations we take to love, serve, and give into the lives of those we care about. Relationships are very much like bank accounts. If we make more withdrawals than deposits, the relationship goes bankrupt. A little extra effort makes additional deposits and generates an amazing return on those investments to be enjoyed by everybody involved.

Relationships need attention just as cars need oil. If you refuse to put oil in your car long enough, you'll find yourself driving with the oil light on and the engine knocking. At this point, most people are not only willing to add oil but also eager to do so. The problem is that once it comes to this point, it's a little too late. So many relationships land in trouble looking for an easy "just add oil" fix. Checking the oil and making sure it stays near the "full line" are well worth the ongoing effort it requires.

Healthy relationships embrace purposeful routines that provide steady nourishment and overall health to any connection. Tracy and I are committed to a Monday night date. This is the least interrupted night of our week, and we give it to each other. Rarely is our Monday night date interrupted, but when it is, we work to ensure the following week is reserved.

Over many years of serving Jesus, loving my wife, giving myself to my family, and devoting time, money, and energy to God's desires to strengthen the church, I've learned something about faithfulness. God measures faithfulness in years. I'm completely capable of being way too hard on myself as are most readers who will pick up this book.

It's in every one of us to feel like we could have done more to become more. This is a terrible enemy to faithfulness. Once we grow discouraged, we are more likely to give up on the overall pursuit of faithfulness. In a moment of inspiration, we make new commitments; some of which I hope will come from reading this book. Instead of growing frustrated or disappointed because of how the week or the month has gone in your new efforts to live a deeper, more meaningful life, just pick up where you left off. Let the next year be the best year you've ever had regardless of how a few days, weeks, or even months out of the year may be lacking.

Staying encouraged is an important part of keeping your motivation to faithfully add the extra to the ordinary in your pursuit of a deeper, more meaningful life. Sometimes it's the beginning steps that can be the most difficult. Skepticism of those who have known you can be a great discouragement if we're not careful.

Zack heard the message on how important it is to date your mate. Immediately, his inspiration was converted into an action plan. To Angie's surprise that Friday night, Zack appeared at the front door holding flowers and smelling of cologne, with a remarkable smile across his face. He even rang the doorbell just like his pastor mentioned to add an extra special touch. Angie stood there holding the doorknob and looking at Zack in stunned silence. Finally, she slammed the door in his face and ran to the phone. Calling the pastor on the phone, she exclaimed, "Pastor, get over here now! Zack just showed up to the house drunk!"

Starting new routines takes some work. But once routines begin to be established, the example is contagious. We are all influenced by what our friends are "into." If our friends are into sports, we develop a greater awareness of sports. If our friends are into building a home, we start considering the house we live in. If our friends are into expanding their family, we begin discussing children more seriously.

Once we break the barrier of a new routine, it affects the people around us. The Bible describes the progression of getting past barriers and excuses, providing an example for others to follow.

Prov 15:19 reads, "The way of the sluggard is blocked with thorns, but the path of the upright is a highway" (NIV).

Early African converts to Christianity were earnest and regular in private devotions. Each one reportedly had a separate spot in the thicket where he would pour out his heart to God. Over time, the paths to these places became well worn, encouraging others to keep their focus in places and paths of prayer. On the contrary, if one of these believers began to neglect prayer, it was soon apparent to the others. They would kindly remind the negligent one, "Brother, the grass grows on your path.[1]"

Just start somewhere and purpose to establish faithfulness of making the ordinary into extraordinary over the years. You'll be amazed at how rich your legacy becomes as a result of steady, continual deposits in the lives of those around you. Deeper, more meaningful lives come from discovering that relationship is the true currency of life. Meaningful and considerate gestures to serve each other turn ordinary situations into extraordinary memories, producing a legacy of great treasure.

When our daughters were born, I was right there with camera in hand capturing their first cries on video. I just

---

[1] "The Grass Grows on Your Path," *Today in the Word*, June 29, 1992

happened to have the camera rolling the precise moment to capture Faith's, our first daughter, first steps on video. Immediately, I began to pray and ask God to arrange this same experience for our next child when that time would come. Amazingly enough, that day came and I actually captured that moment in Lexi's, our younger daughter, life as well.

My calendar had a monthly reminder to write a journal to my girls. Each month of their lives growing up, I would write a simple expression of something unique I'd noticed in that season of their lives and include a few pictures in the entry. As the girls approached twelve years old, I had over one hundred pages of posts with pictures embedded in the text.

We had these pages bound together with a cover sheet from a local copy shop. In the beginning, I had no idea what this would become. Over time, I realized that it was something very special. When my daughters were ready for purity rings, I took them on a very special and very formal daddy–daughter date, just the two of us. This involved going to pick up flowers and ringing the doorbell like a gentleman would. Picking up my date, we went to a very special place. During the date, I presented them with the bound journal and a purity ring.

In both situations, minutes turned to hours as we looked through the pages sitting in the restaurant beside each other. The meal, though exquisite, seemed insignificant as we experienced greater nourishment that God inspired Moses to write about and later Jesus would reiterate, "Man does not live on bread alone." The ordinary in our lives had become extraordinary in that moment as we reflected together on simple entries like this one:

July 7th, 2005

Dear Faith,

You really blessed me this week in a very special way. We were in a swimming pool and you were calling me over to you. There were several people there and you had been watching me do flips on the diving board and mess with people as I was joking around. I noticed your little finger krinkling as I looked at you and you were doing the "come here" motion with a really sweet look on your face.

I made my way to you as you were floating in the water with your little arm floaties on. I got to you and you asked me to come close so you could whisper something to me. I leaned down to you and you put your hand beside my ear whispering, "You're my hero."

I almost cried it meant so very much to me. You are such a sweet girl. I hope you always think I'm your hero.

Dad

TREAURES WITHIN YOUR REACH

WHEN **J**ESUS **CAME** teaching in Matt 10:7 that the kingdom of God is at hand, I believe he was revealing that life's greatest treasures are within our reach. It's so easy to simply be consumed by life, allowing the most important things to slip away. One of the most common phrases we parents say is, "They grow up so fast!" Making the most of every stage of life and family is very important and simply involves purposeful and deliberate appreciation and involvement.

She was nine years old and could hardly concentrate at school. Tonight was her special date with her daddy. The clock seemed to be in slow motion that day, but finally, the concluding bell sounded. She rushed home to get just the right outfit. Her instructions to her daddy were very specific for that night, "suit and tie!" It was going to be a special evening out, just the two of them.

Finally, the time arrived; it was 5:45. Her daddy appeared from his room in his nicest suit. As suddenly as he appeared, he was gone slipping out through the garage. It would take fifteen minutes to make it around the corner to buy flowers and return. This time, the car wasn't pulled into the garage. Her daddy wanted to demonstrate the behavior of a true gentleman. The car was left waiting in the driveway as the doorbell rang. The door opened and the daughter's smile was more than a facial expression. This smile came all the way from the heart.

Flowers, escort to the car, door opened for the lady, the music just right at her preference, and the inquiry "Are you hot, cold, or just right?" are all done as what a real man's behavior should be. There will be boys who will try to enter her life in days ahead. The counterfeits will be easily identified because of the experience of what a deeper, more meaningful life is all about on her daddy–daughter dates.

These dates aren't trips to exotic places around the world. These are average places to sit, talk, and laugh. After the evening ends, it's hardly even possible to describe the topics that created such laughter because it really wasn't ever about the topics just as it wasn't about the food.

One day, I was busy working in my home office. Tracy wasn't due home for another hour, so I decided to create a memory with my girls. It was near the Christmas holiday, so taking my camera in hand, I coached our two young daughters through the Christmas story. Costumes were crude and the acting required bribing with cookies, but we did it! The video was such a hit that year on Christmas Day as we watched it with family and at our office parties; we decided to make it an annual tradition.

Baking cookies and delivering them to somebody as a family will enrich your home in amazing ways. Shopping for groceries for somebody in need becomes a tremendous lesson in giving and the blessing associated with it. Instead of letting time pass you by, make the choice to create memories.

A Christ-centered, loving, serving, and giving culture in your life, family, and home will not happen just because you hope it happens. Hope is not a strategy. This takes work, planning, dedication, and even accountable relationships with others who have the same goal in mind.

It takes discipline to purpose a family meal where there is no distraction and conversation is the main course. I'll never forget the evening at our dinner table when I announced that the Holy Spirit was convicting me of having my phone on at the table. It's constantly dinging and ringing with somebody demanding my attention away from my family. I was shocked as I barely finished making this announcement that the girls literally applauded with cheers of celebration. It was an impacting moment for me as I realized how cheated my children obviously felt. They were seeing me being somebody else's hero when I needed to be their daddy during those routinely nourishing family moments.

Learning the value of the simple things in life produces deeper, more meaningful memories. Distractions are justifiable and can even find their way into endorsement and understanding of those who are being cheated around you. My family tends to be very understanding when I'm fielding calls and situations where people need pastoral counsel and support. My girls are all too familiar with the two-finger motion dragging my fingers below my eyes to indicate I'm talking to somebody who is crying. This means *Please leave the room so I can have a personal conversation with somebody in need.*

The situation, regardless of their level of enthusiasm to share something exciting with their dad, turns to the disposition of disappointment when they observe the invisible barrier. It may be invisible, but it definitely exists and communicates the off-limits nature of my attention span. What is your barrier? Perhaps it's your work, your hobbies, other relationships, entertainment, or any other justifiable distraction from the deeper, more meaningful things in your life.

If we neglect what is within our reach, it's only a matter of time before the most important things in life have slipped away. It's less costly and more rewarding to invest in a marriage than to suffer divorce. It's less costly and more rewarding to invest time with children than to suffer the disconnection of angry teens justifying their repayment of the painful sting of neglect. What is within your reach that you need to assign a greater priority? It's never too late to make an improvement, and giving God something to work with might completely turn things around.

Moses stood alone, having lost all hope of his dreams. God gets his attention and asks him this profoundly important question, "What's in your hand?" The key to his future was clearly within his reach. What was in his hand didn't look like the dream in his heart.

What is within your reach is there because God gives us something to work with. We can easily get so enamored with the dreams in our heart that we lose sight of what God's placed within our reach. For Moses, it was his rod. For an unnamed boy in the New Testament, it was his five loaves and two fish. Learning to value what's in our hand unlocks an entirely new dimension of life.

Jesus didn't come so that we might have and enjoy vacation. He came so that we might have and enjoy life. We endure life and look forward to having and enjoying vacation. It's not the vacation dream that brings the greatest joy. It's the life that's in our reach every day that God desires for us to treasure.

The moment was just right for the exciting announcement, "We're going to Disney World!" Excitement filled the room! With weeks to go after the announcement before meeting Mickey and his friends, conversation around the table was dominated by expectations of amazing fun! Every time we had a meal, a discussion would erupt about all the things we were going to do when we finally get there.

Finally, it was time. Through the airport, we ran to catch our plane. Upon landing, we gathered our luggage and were off to get the rental car. Arriving at the hotel, we got checked in and were ready for the big day. The next morning, we were going to experience Disney World! We were finally there.

The morning came, and we all got up much more readily than a typical school day. We drove into the lot to discover it would cost fourteen dollars to park. Once in the lot, we drove further and further away from the front gate past an ocean of parked cars to find a spot, but finally, we were there. Everybody jumped out of the car because we could see the parking lot tram was about to leave. Can you believe it? We missed it!

At last, another tram arrived to take us to the gate. Credit cards were waving, tickets were exchanging, and we were waiting behind it all. One family at a time but it was finally our turn, and after paying a good portion of the kids' college fund, *finally we were there!*

Rides, shows, bathrooms, and, finally, the lunch stop! I gazed at the menu as the first item to capture my attention was spaghetti and meatballs for only $15.99! What a day of "having fun!" It blazed by leaving us numb and exhausted in the room that night.

Maybe it was that night in the hotel that I realized the place of family enjoyment wasn't actually Disney World. As odd as it sounds, it's true. We could go back to that dinner table the first night we made the announcement and *we were already there*. It's all too easy to miss the obvious treasures and pleasures in life.

Relying on Disney World for family fun is like relying on cotton candy for nutrition.

Losing sight of what's important causes us to look past wonderful treasures that can be embraced in every moment of life. This vain pursuit of fulfillment leaves us socially malnourished, confused, and frustrated. To think we must travel the world to enjoy family time is a lie. To effectively embrace what is within our reach, we must view life from God's relational priorities.

Erma Bombeck wrote more than four thousand newspaper columns. When asked if she would do anything different if she had life to live over again, she stated the following in her book:[2]

> If I had my life to live over again I would have waxed less and listened more. Instead of wishing away nine months of pregnancy and complaining about the shadows over my feet, I would have cherished every

2   Erma Bombeck, *Forever, Erma: Best-Loved Writing From America's Favorite Humorist* (Kansas City: Andrews McMeel Publishing, 1997)

minute of it and realize that the wonderment growing inside of me was to be my only chance in life
to assist God in a miracle. I would have never have
insisted that the car windows be rolled up on a sum-
mer day because my hair had just been teased and
sprayed. I would have invited friends over to dinner
even if the carpet was stained and the sofa faded. I
would have eaten popcorn in the good living room
and worried less about the dirt when you lit the fire-
place. I would have taken the time to listen to my
grandfather ramble about his youth. I would have
burnt the paint candle sculptured like a rose before
it melted while being stored in the garage. I would
have sat cross-legged on the lawn with my children and never worried about grass stains. I would
have cried & laughed less while watching television
and more while watching life. I would have shared
more of the responsibilities carried by my husband
which I took for granted. I would have eaten less
cottage cheese and more ice cream. I would have
never bought anything just because it was practi-
cal. When my child kissed me impetuously I would
never have said, 'Later; now go up and get washed
for dinner.' There would have been more 'I love you's'
and more 'I'm sorries' and more 'I am listening.' But
more than that, if I was given another shot at life I
would seize every moment of it. Try it on. Live it.
Exhaust it until there was nothing left of it.

Jesus came and gave his life so we could have life. Don't squander it away by being distracted from life's greatest treasures, which are clearly within your reach! Make the time to value and appreciate the more important things in life. Treasure those things. Remember those things.

2.15.2007

Dear Lexi,

Mommy told me that while I was away this past weekend you guys had a great time all together. Faith was reading with great expression and you were listening and demanding to see the pictures. The evening apparently unfolded as a wonderful time together for you three girls.

At one point you, perhaps noticing Faith's expression, said, "Mommy this is my shy face." You tucked your chin and acted coy. A few days later I asked if you would show me your shy face. You immediately put on this expression. I then requested a few more like happy, surprised and sad. To each request you gave an immediate response. Finally you said, "God gave me all those faces." We cracked up. I'm glad you know where your resources have come from in life. I'm also glad that you are allowing him to be in charge of how you use those resources.

Love you much! You're a hoot!

Dad

TIME SPELLS HONOR

IN A WORLD that is over-committed and under-connected, we must fight for quality family time. This fight is a biblical fight to honor God and to honor your family above other things and above yourself. It's amazing what God makes happen for us when we make things happen for others. The pursuit of happiness tends to be about how I can spend my time working at being happy. The pursuit of blessedness tends to be about how I can spend my time investing in and blessing others. Somehow the pursuit of blessedness achieves for me what the pursuit of happiness never could.

Rom 12:10 states, "Be devoted to one another in brotherly love. Honor one another above yourselves" (NIV).

Interestingly, the Greek word that translates *honor* is actually spelled *time* in the Greek language. There is no greater priority we can assign to others than the assignment of our time. Money is a resource that can be replenished if spent foolishly. Once our time is spent, it's no longer recoverable. We are allotted a certain number of years, months, weeks, days, hours, minutes, and seconds, and then our lives on this earth will come to an end.

To honor God and to honor my family, I resolved that I would devote myself to embrace every season of life wholeheartedly to the best of my ability. It takes discipline not to merely rush through one season of life with another season in mind. Each season is a purposed time from God to be honored, appreciated, valued, and embraced.

After twenty-three years of marriage, the time had come. We'd been faithfully saving, and now, Tracy and I were ready to build our dream home. We'd been searching for a few years and finally gave up on buying so we were building. Our two girls were almost in their teens, and we wanted them to have wonderful memories in their home before moving away to college. We discovered a wonderful two-acre lot that was heavily wooded. It was settled; this was the spot! We were introduced to a man who could clear the area for the pad of the house and his work began. I stood taking video of the first tree that fell. Excitement filled the car as we drove away leaving him to his work. It would be about six hours later when I received the call voicing confusion about the task.

Driving my daughters back out to the lot, we saw that much work had been accomplished. The lot looked terribly different now with a huge pile of trees at one end. As the discussion began, my heart started racing and I could feel the emotion begin to rise like a volcano ready to erupt. What?! Are you serious?! Somehow the man got turned around, and instead of clearing the lot so the house would face north, he cleared the lot so the house would face west. My emotional gaskets blew as I was standing there processing the money wasted and the dream destroyed.

Ultimately, it would all work out, but at that moment, I didn't know this and my emotions were running high. I went to bed that night feeling terrible about myself. The next morning, I woke up and the Holy Spirit gently spoke to me that I needed to move from the task of building a house to the experience of building a home with my family as part of our life experience together.

That week, I bought a chainsaw. Every family member was issued a pair of work gloves. We went out to cut limbs, knowing we'd not make a hint of a dent; but we did it for the homebuilding memory as a family. Taking the time to enjoy the journey is a very important part of life. It's not just spending time in the same vicinity, but it's being disciplined to invest quality time focused on the people God has entrusted to our care in an engaged and deliberate fashion.

There really is a difference between merely making a living and truly making a life.

Every year, as a pastor, I stand with many couples who are devoting their lives together in marriage. The progression is always the same. With great excitement and enthusiasm, the young couple gets engaged. Tension and pressure begin to mount as the day draws near, and the total focus tends to be the wedding ceremony. My responsibility is to bring their focus and attention beyond preparing for the wedding to what it takes to prepare for the marriage.

The preparation is rigorous because marriage takes work. The wedding immediately captivates the focus of everybody surrounding the newly engaged couple. The problem is that the wedding will come and go and it's the marriage that must remain. My premarital counseling requires young couples to read four books with meetings after the book assignments are complete. We write a mission statement, work on a budget, discuss effective communication, talk about where to spend Thanksgiving and Christmas, how many children will come about when, who cleans, who cooks, and what intimacy is really all about in the relationship.

It takes time to effectively plan for something as meaningful as abundant life. If we're not careful, we grow distracted from meaningful investments. God is always stretching us into a deeper, more meaningful plan that is filled with eternal significance. Today really isn't about today. My life isn't even about my life. An honorable life is a life that invests time in purposes beyond simply getting all "I want" out of "my life."

Living purposefully takes us from merely spending time to truly investing it. Our job is what we're paid to do, but our work is what we're born to do. It's easy to get locked into the vicious cycle of earning, spending, eating, and sleeping. The spending medicates the disappointment resulting from a lack of purpose, which requires us to work harder to earn more. Before we know it, we've lost ourselves in meaningless existence where time and money just pass by and slip away.

There is a very well-known adage, "Time flies when you're having fun." Our culture has become so entertainment centered that it's no wonder life is so fleeting. Adolescence is now extended well beyond the teen years as corporations have successfully developed the art of servicing "kidults." Adults who are held hostage with childhood interests make great customers and easy prey to profit-pursuing companies who gladly keep you entertained and self-absorbed. This keeps you spending your money and your time "having fun."

We carry in our pockets, in the shape of a phone, the potential capacity to waste our entire lives. So many men and women in their twenties are nowhere near ready to live responsibly, invest in a marriage, or inspire children to live deeper, more meaningful lives. According to statistics, the average high school student, by the time they graduate, will have spent more time watching television than attending school. The average single guy, depending upon what survey you believe, spends between three and four hours a day playing video games.

Our culture has become so obsessed with being entertained that it's no wonder life is so fleeting. Just because fast food fills your stomach doesn't mean it's nourishing your body. We are a generation that knows how to be served well. Unfortunately, the key to a deeper, more meaningful life has more to do with serving others than it does with having people serve us. The problem with the rat race is that the winner is still just a rat.

Every life ends with the same conclusion. There are always two dates and a dash. The dash gets very little attention, as the beginning and the end seem to be the focus. It's interesting how this resembles our lives. There is a lot of attention at the beginning and, again, at the end. Only those who are closest to us through the years of our lives know what that dash really stood for. The years that actually mattered!

The problem is that the "dash" explains how we tend to live those years. We dash here and we dash there. We dash everywhere, rushing through the days of our pressurized lives! One day, I noticed a continual command I gave to my six- and seven-year-old daughters. Over one of our weekly family meals, I shared how I was no longer going to say "Hurry up!" I was amazed at how challenging this was.

When I needed to get the family moving toward the car to be on time, I would start to say the forbidden phrase. Suddenly, I would catch myself and would rework the phrase to communicate the same thing, only using different terminology. Then I began to realize just how deeply rooted our rushed lives are with subtle messages everywhere. To lose weight, you can buy slim fast. When you need a forgotten grocery item, you can stop at a Quick Mart. There are ten-minute tans, Federal Express, and you can even swim in a Speedo!

The message is constant, and our minds are conditioned to rush through life. Life is better when we slow down and take the time to remember that what we are doing is not as important as who we're doing it with.

An experiment was conducted with students at Princeton Theological Seminary[3]. Students were informed that they would be recorded when speaking on an assigned topic in another building. On the pathway, they would walk and the students encountered a "victim" slumped in a doorway. Half of the students were assigned to talk on the good Samaritan parable. Some were told they were late and should hurry, some were told they had just enough time to

---

[3] Darley, JM and Batson, CD, "'From Jerusalem to Jericho': A study of situational and dispositional variables in help-ing ehavior," *Journal of Personality and Social Psychology* 27 (1973).

get to the recording room, and some were told they would arrive early.

The variable that made a difference was how much of a hurry they were in. Sixty-three percent of those who were in no hurry stopped to help, forty-five percent of those in a moderate hurry stopped, and ten percent of those that were in a great hurry stopped. It made no difference whether the students were assigned to talk on the good Samaritan parable.

The way we structure our schedules has a profound impact on how we translate beliefs into behavior.

We have no indication from the Scripture that Jesus ever rushed from place to place trying to fit everything in. Yet the weight of the world truly was resting upon his shoulders. Somehow he was able to effectively respond to interruptions without neglecting purposeful opportunities in those unexpected moments of time. How do you respond to people when they interrupt your busy schedule? This question has forced me to face a painful reality in my own life. However, being honest about our weakness is not the only way we receive help but it's also the way we mentor others effectively.

May 13, 2006

Wow! What A Date!!! Every week I take mommy out for our date. Yesterday she had a dental procedure and wasn't feeling very well afterward. We were actually attending a very formal banquet. You volunteered to go so I discussed with Lexi. I told her how I would take her out for a very special night soon if she was okay with your going in mommy's place to this event.

I went to the store and got flowers and came to knock on the door to pick up my date. You and Lexi were both so excited to receive flowers. Then you and I whisked off in the car. As we drove down the street you were so cute as you started working to impress your date. From nowhere you said, "I know what 2 + 2 is… 4." Then you said, "I know what 3+3 is…" I inquired and you began frantically counting your fingers to come up with "6". I was so proud to be somebody you wanted to impress.

We went to a very formal banquet hall in downtown OKC surrounded by huge buildings. You had on a beautiful dress and silk gloves. You were definitely the talk of the banquet. You were so big sitting there following all the rules of dinner etiquette. We left early and drove through all of the big buildings downtown with the top down on the car. You were in awe and I was absolutely thrilled! You finally said, "I wish Lexi were here!" I thought it was so special. Thanks for an amazing time.

MEN-TOURS

MY FAMILY AND I were on our way out of town. For whatever reason, my attitude was lacking that day, and I found myself being short with everybody. In one instance, I snapped at my five-year-old daughter who sat in the back of the van processing her daddy's insensitive attitude. Suddenly, I pulled over and asked if she would unbuckle and come to the front. The look of fear on her face said it all, and I was sure her mom and little sister debated intervening.

She climbed up in the front seat and sat on my lap, and then I looked deeply into her eyes. My eyes began to fill with tears as I told her that I was very aware that I'd been having a bad attitude and that my comment to her was simply not pleasing to God. With sincerity, I asked my little girl, "Would you please forgive me?" We both sat there crying at this point, and she hugged me with affirmation, restoration, and healing. I've never forgotten that moment, and hopefully, I never will.

An unkind attitude in the parent fosters an unkind atmosphere in the home. Everybody struggles with their attitude at times, but that doesn't give anybody the right to require others to just deal with it. As parents, we can get away with moving on and ignoring the collateral damage. The problem is that the damage exists in the form of seeds and will grow into outbursts of disrespect, then to eruptions of resentment.

When you blow it, don't compound the mistake by covering it up and carrying on as if nothing happened. Say "I'm sorry" as sincerely as you can, and let God be in charge of damage control. It's amazing what he can do with a sincere apology.

Mentoring others is allowing men to tour our life. If we never allow them to tour our failures, they'll be disillusioned. This alleviates the pressure of trying to pretend we are something we are not. Fake presentation is shallow and is one of the most destructive ideas to a deeper, more meaningful life.

Monterey, CA, was a pelican's paradise. Fishermen cleaned their fish, leaving the entrails for pelicans to enjoy. Birds grew fat and lazy. At some point, this ceased as creative entrepreneurialism found a use for these innards. Pelicans began starving to death because they had grown up with parent pelicans that didn't teach them how to fish. They actually imported pelicans that could demonstrate this skill, and soon, the famine was ended.[4]

St. Francis of Assisi said, "Preach the Gospel. And if necessary, use words." What we do speaks volumes more than what we say. Our lives are influencing other people, and we must take responsibility for this reality!

Once I heard a man talking about how he would teach horses to cross bridges. Young horses would be scared to cross a bridge until they'd been tied to older horses which had crossed them before. Following the lead of the older horse, the younger horse would easily cross and learn to do so by himself. This speaks of how we are to be examples to others, enabling them to go into territory of their lives where they simply wouldn't go if we weren't there leading the way.

Being a great example is actually one of the most confusing ideas in our faith. Jesus is the only perfect example. We can never be a great example until we stop trying to be a perfect one. Imperfection in our lives is actually helpful to others. Our mistakes are part of our example of God's forgiveness to others. God takes just a man and makes him a just man, but he's still just a man.

Fake people aren't real, and real people aren't fake. We are not merely a carrier of the message of Christ. We are the message, and our mistakes are a necessary part of the

---

[4]   *Bits & Pieces*, June 23, 1994, p. 17.

message of our lives. Healthy apologies produce life in any relationship. *Never mess up a perfectly good apology with an excuse.* We all make mistakes, and taking ownership of our mistakes is part of getting past them.

Everybody has hesitation when we think about being used by God! I call it the "Who Me Syndrome," and it's prevalent in the Bible. Abraham thought he was too old. Mary thought she was too young. Moses thought he didn't speak well enough. Gideon thought he was too scared. David was ready, but nobody else seemed to think so.

The truth is that God blesses who we are. He won't bless the person who we think we should be. He won't bless the person people try to make us to be. God always blesses the seed to produce the harvest. Rarely does the seed resemble the harvest. Learning to be confident and comfortable as you are is a very important part of serving the Lord and participating with his gracious blessing.

If you don't understand this concept, you will constantly disqualify yourself from God's plan for your life. Augustine said, "Without God, man cannot, but without man, God will not."

God's plans being released in our world depend on our willingness to be ourselves and fulfill our God-given assignments. God's not anointing who you think you should be or what others tell you to be. God's anointing who he made you to be. Most of us have been taught to present an example. God's more authentic than that! Being yourself is the first step to becoming what God designed you to be.

If you are going to be effective, you have to be authentic. If you try to live for the approval of others, you'll always be stressed out for fear of being discovered.

Prov 29:25 says, "Fear of man will prove to be a snare, but whoever trusts in the Lord is kept safe" (NIV).

Prov 14:26 reads, "Fear of the Lord is a strong confidence" (KJV).

You are not designed to live with an unhealthy fear of man. It's easy to play the popularity game. Once I had the privilege of meeting John Maxwell. I was speaking in a conference, and he'd been invited to be the keynote speaker. As we snacked in the speakers' hospitality area, I introduced myself. He used my name several times in the conversation to practice remembering my name. Later, he saw me and called me by first name.

After the conference, I received in the mail a leadership CD from John Maxwell to which I'd subscribed for a few years. As the CD arrived, I felt a sense of personal relational connection now that my friend, John, knew my name. My sense of success was slightly inflated because I was on a first name basis with the best-selling author John Maxwell. As I began driving away from my office that day, listening to John's message, it started out this way, "Learn the names of insignificant people. It will mean a lot to them." Hilarious! I'd fallen prey to the insignificant crowd in John's life.

It was such a great lesson for me in life. Relax. Be who you are. Don't try to impress others but just trust in who God designed you to be every day that you live. Luther said, "God doesn't love us because we're valuable. We're valuable because God loves us." God's love in our messed-up lives is the message of the Gospel.

God didn't hide any of the dirty laundry in the Bible. This causes the Bible to stand alone in a class all its own as no other religion allows humanity to be exposed in their book.

Jesus's family lineage is a mess for all to see in Matthew 1, as the New Testament begins. His mom wasn't married. His great, great grandma Rahab was a prostitute. His great, great grandpa David had an adulterous affair and attempted to cover it up with murder. The Bible reveals strength, weakness, pain, and purpose in the lives of anybody listed. Joseph was abused by his family and forgotten by his leadership. Abraham was too old. Leah was unattractive. Moses stuttered. Jonah was slow to respond. Elijah was suicidal. Peter was hot-tempered. Martha was a worrier. Thomas had doubts. This mess is clearly revealed for all to see and understand that God sent Jesus into our mess to turn it into a message, because he is the MESSiah.

Don't let your issues be your excuses. The good news for all of us is that God uses dysfunctional people. You are not merely a carrier of the message. Your mess is part of the message. People who know you can believe God might actually be able to use them if he can use you. 1 Cor 1:27 teaches us how God has chosen the "foolish" things of the world to shame the wise and the weak things of the world to shame the strong.

The Greek word for "foolish" is *moros*, from which we get the word *morons*. God's looking for morons! Our failures are directly tied to our success. We fail more than we succeed, so our ability to handle failure is directly tied to our ability to succeed.

Andrew Carnegie said, "Finding greatness in an individual is a lot like mining for gold. When you go into the mine you realize that you will have to move a ton of dirt to find an ounce of gold. However, you never go to the mine looking for the dirt. You always go to the mine looking for the gold!"

Tracy and I went shopping for a leather couch once. As we were looking, we noticed a distressed leather couch. There was a tag on this beautiful couch that said something like, "All of the markings, scarring and discolorations on this product are normal and enhance its natural beauty."

As I read this, I pondered how the tag might read on our lives. It's probably something like this: "This person is not faulty or damaged. All the markings, scarring, and blemishes are normal and enhance the humanity and authenticity of a life lived in pursuit of the purposes of God."

It's as obvious as it is offensive that the Scripture reveals how Jesus didn't spend time with good people. He spent time with real people. Many people get real and surrender their broken lives to him. The problem comes as they start trying to cover the brokenness when they're taught the religious ideas of being good and "acting" how a Christian should. Somewhere along the journey, they stop being real. Being real is something we all have to work at on a daily basis. This is the only way to experience true freedom, and it will become contagious in the lives of others as we are transparent about our struggles.

James 5:16 reads, "Therefore confess your sins to each other and pray for each other so that you may be healed. The prayer of a righteous man is powerful and effective" (NIV). Notice that it's the confessing of our sins openly which triggers healing as we pray in honesty about our weakness and sin. I love that the verse concludes by emphasizing how a righteous man's prayer is powerful and effective when it's obviously referencing somebody who has confessed sin. Righteous men and women of God are those who have discovered that the cross of Jesus will cover whatever we are willing to uncover in our lives. It's what we leave covered in our lives that the cross will never cover.

Over the years, I've had the privilege of meeting a lot of pastors. It's always a privilege to meet the men and women who serve God's family in our local community. The conversations are typically genuine but somewhat guarded as we are all inclined to express success and happiness regardless of what kind of painful situations we may be walking through. One day, that changed as I passed by a pastor acquaintance and extended the basic greeting, asking how he was. His response shocked me.

Clutching my hand for what was more than a mere handshake, he looked transparently into my eyes and said, "I'm not doing very well. Can we talk?" In that moment, he shared how hearing me speak at a recent speaking engagement in the community made him want to open up to me. I'd shared how I'd been on drugs, was a heavy metal lead guitarist in '80s rock bands, and how meeting Jesus changed my life.

My willingness to openly share my embarrassing past stirred an appetite in this wonderful man who was silently struggling with an addiction of his own. We began to talk openly, and from that moment on, our relationship had roots of true friendship that hadn't existed before. When we focus on our strengths, it breeds competition. When we focus on our weakness, it breeds community. A deeper, more meaningful life is the result of transparency and community. This is the foundation upon which God builds our lives and the basis for true friendship.

July 16th, 2008

This morning you girls asked to go with me as I was leaving early to go to my favorite prayer spot. We went and sat reading a few verses. We talked about what God was revealing through our reading and then we went to the park to play. Quality time with God doesn't have to be some long drawn out difficult thing. We spent the morning having fun in the park, talking about and implementing the truth we discussed about how God knows the motives of our hearts.

When we got into the car Faith said, "When I have children I'm going to bring them to this very prayer spot as my favorite place to pray where my daddy brought me." Then she explained how her kids would do the same with their kids and if they didn't she was going to get onto them. I laughed pretty hard but it really struck a chord with me to say the least!

BIBLICAL BLUEPRINT

THE BLUEPRINT SPEAKS of all the forethought that goes into building a building or a home. Somebody meticulously went over important details and then made those details clear so that what is being built is well constructed. The Bible is that blueprint for our lives.

Biblically impoverished people live poorly constructed lives.

In 1989, a terrible earthquake rocked the San Francisco Bay Area on October 17 at 5:04 p.m. local time. The quake measured 7.0 on the Richter scale and tragically killed sixty-three people.[5] In 2010, a terrible earthquake hit Haiti on January 12 at 4:53 p.m. local time. The quake also meas-

---

[5]   Eberhart-Phillips JE, Saunders TM, Robinson AL, Hatch DL, Parrish RG, "Profile of mortality from the 1989 Loma Prieta earthquake using coroner and medical examiner reports," *Disasters* 18 (2) (June 1994): 160–70.

ured 7.0 on the Richter scale, but in this instance, sixty-three people weren't killed. Horribly, more than 230,000 people were killed.[6]

How can the same magnitude of an earthquake in two heavily populated locations have completely different fatality conclusions? One very obvious reason is the impoverished people of Haiti live and work in poorly constructed structures compared to the engineered structures in San Francisco. The level of suffering and agony was exponentially multiplied because of the poor construction.

The level of construction clearly influences the level of suffering and loss in catastrophic times. God has given forethought to constructing our lives beyond our wildest imagination. The level of construction depends upon our willingness to cooperate with the biblical blueprint he's made readily available. Biblically impoverished people live poorly constructed lives.

In reverse, biblically inspired people live better-constructed lives. A biblical blueprint reveals the ministry center to be the home for the Jews. It's unfortunate that we have allowed the ministry center for Christians to primarily be the church. This is a clear discrepancy from the blueprint God has provided. The church is a very important part of our faith but should be an extension of our primary ministry from our homes. Bringing the life of the Scripture

---

[6] "Haiti quake death toll rises to 230,000" (article from *BBC*, February 10, 2010).

into every day living fosters an amazingly healthy atmosphere for any household.

My daughters, ages eleven and twelve, were unimpressed with my morning antics on this particular morning. I had been up and awake for a while and had broken through the personal morning barrier we all experience. My girls, however, had only just started to see the barrier ahead of them. Their slow and sluggish movement was met with my energized attitude.

My older daughter, Faith, looked at me and said, "Dad! Please! The Bible says do not provoke your children!" Realizing I'd come very near violating this biblical caution in the Scripture of which Faith was keenly aware, I was extra cooperative. With sincere apology, I expressed, "I'm sorry girls. I've also read where the Bible says not to greet people with a loud voice in the morning." To which my younger daughter, Lexi, replied, "Read it again, Dad. Read it again."

Perhaps this was the funniest moment of that entire month. We rehearsed it several times laughing about the comment. The more I thought about it, the more thrilled I was that my children are quoting the Bible to me now. Lord knows I need it!

The natural order of life tends to be reduced to mere existence and surviving circumstances. God designed us for far more than existence. His plan is that we truly live! Jesus spoke of this incredible blueprint for truly living in John 10.

John 10:10 reads, "I came that they may have and enjoy life, and have it in abundance (to the full, till it overflows)" (Amplified).

The problem is that there is a natural force working against this life. This natural force is seen in the winding down of all energy in our world. Science refers to this as the law of entropy. Every car I've ever purchased is continually winding down. Over the years, I discovered it is slowly falling apart. This is the natural order of our world, and if I'm not constantly investing in and maintaining to re-energize this winding down entity of a car, it will ultimately fall apart.

The natural order of all things in our world is to wind down. Marriages wind down. Friendships wind down. Families wind down. There is a need to invest in and maintain every entity that is winding down. Marriages need both people to invest in and maintain the marriage relationship. Jesus invested in and maintains our relationship as our example of how to invest in and maintain other relationships. With sacrificial love, he surrendered his glorious position on a throne and served the needs of fallen humanity on a cross.

Serving, loving, and giving are the blueprint Jesus gave us to invest in and maintain marriages, friendships, and relationships in general. There is nothing more wonderful than two servants in love. There is nothing more painful than two selfish people in a marriage. The biblical blueprint for true life is one that considers the needs, wants, and desires of others.

Dale Carnegie accurately stated, "You can make more friends in two months by becoming interested in other people than you can in two years by trying to get other people interested in you." Our cultural pursuit of happiness is based on selfishness. A biblical pursuit of blessedness is based on selflessness. This biblical blueprint is counterintuitive in many ways. The pursuit of blessedness is all about loving, serving, and giving to others. The pursuit of blessedness will do more for you than the pursuit of happiness ever could.

People don't set out to build selfish lives. It's just the natural order of the world to do so. Unless you wage war against what comes naturally, it will quietly control you. In all situations, there is a battle that takes place before the behavior. Our decisions determine our destiny, and it's the inconspicuous decisions that have produced the obvious results in our lives.

If we are to address the obvious results in our lives, we must address them in the inconspicuous places where they were born. Our western culture hails success and productivity as a primary value to possess. Through hard work and years of sacrifice, you can climb the ladder of success. There may be nothing more disappointing in life than to spend years climbing the ladder of success only to discover it was propped against the wrong wall all along.

In our culture, it's common to keep a pace that costs your peace. *We must beware of the barrenness of busy lives!* When we are too busy for people, we are just too busy, and the reality is that high levels of "busyness" hold us captive. It is very intriguing to consider how Jesus structured his life and how he handled interruptions.

The reality is that the majority of Jesus's miracles happened in moments of interruption. It was when he was on a very important mission to rescue a twelve-year-old little girl from dying that he found himself in a crowd of people trying to get to him. Luke 8 describes the crowd to have almost crushed Jesus. In the midst of his important mission trying to get through this forceful crowd, Jesus was interrupted.

Suddenly, as he was trying to get through the people crowding all around him, he stops and asks a seemingly bizarre question. "Who touched me?" (Luke 8:45). On this very important mission, sifting through hundreds of people, Jesus was able to respond with an awareness of what God was doing. It was in this moment of interruption that the woman with the issue of blood would receive her miracle.

As stated in Mark 2, Jesus was teaching in a place that was so packed nobody could get in. A few guys cut a hole in the roof and lowered their friend into the room, interrupting Jesus. In this moment of interruption, Jesus didn't treat the interruption as an interruption. Somehow he saw interruptions as part of his assignment.

How do we handle interruptions in our busy lives? It's not like we have a higher degree of pressure than Jesus did. Here is the Son of God, allotted a total of thirty-three years of life, with only three of those in public ministry. He had an entire world to save, and certainly, he could have bypassed the needs of these situations I've mentioned.

To understand a biblical blueprint for life is to recognize that there is a plan that was in motion before we were born. This is the plan that is most important and must take higher priority than our own personal agendas.

Mark 8:36 says, "For what does it profit a man to gain the whole world, and forfeit his soul?" (NAS).

Just because we're breathing doesn't mean we're living. A biblical blueprint for our lives is one of loving, serving, and giving into the lives of those God has entrusted to our care. Our loving efforts are sometimes met with complication and frustration, but even these can become memories.

11/6/07:

Tracy and the girls were shrieking and screaming from the front of the house. Faith and Lexi come running to find me. "Daddy! Daddy! Hurry! It's a murgency!", they exclaimed.

Naturally I'm reaching for weapons at this point running to the front of the house to see what adventure was taking place without me. The utility room door is shut and the keeper of the door, Tracy, was visibly alarmed. "A wasp is in the house!" Tracy exclaimed. Faith and Lexi squealed.

In my vast wisdom as a father and dad I explained that I knew exactly what to do. Disappearing toward the back I then re-emerged with a can of hairspray in hand. Boldly and bravely I entered the door with my three damsels in distress looking on. Surely they were wondering, "Will he ever come back..." I did find this invasive creature and with one mighty spray he fell to the floor unable to fly. Yes folks–this is the best way to deal with a bee or wasp that gets into your home.

What a great success. It wasn't until this morning that I lost some credibility as the hero of the house. Faith and Lexi were ready for school before Tracy was ready to go. As usual, we go run around in the front yard while waiting. As we were out there I began thinking–surely that wasp wasn't the lone ranger. We began searching and guess what we found? A nest in our outside light fixture. I positioned the girls at a safe distance where they could watch their most confident father demonstrate once again my extermination abilities. Grabbing the wasp spray from the garage I came out and explained to the girls how this spray goes about 20 feet. With great precision I aimed the spray right at the nest and when I pressed the button the can malfunctioned and it sprayed in my left eye—not what a heroic father was expecting. I finally grabbed a broom and knocked the nest down. As my three lovely damsels drove out of the driveway I was over the sink in the bathroom flushing out my eye. Don't try this at home, kids.

RELATIONALLY ENRICHED

WE WENT ON a trip to Florida one year with my wife's entire family. During the course of the trip, we decided to pay for a snorkeling and scuba diving excursion. Since I'm the only one certified to dive, I went exploring with a guide while everybody else snorkeled. In the midst of the fascination of beautiful coral, I noticed a large shadow. Turning, I saw that I was less than twenty feet from a large hammerhead. As you can imagine, I wondered if I would ever surface that day, swimming next to this eight- to nine-foot-long shark.

The shark slowly swam past us going the opposite direction, and I'm sure he was evaluating the buffet. Looking ahead to my guide, I realized he hadn't even seen the shark. As I continually tried to signal danger, he never knew what

I was signaling about. I spent the next fifteen minutes looking over my shoulder fearing that at any given moment, I would lose a leg like the book *Jaws* described in its first shark incident.

I started processing the thrill of this experience, thinking how I couldn't wait to get back to the surface to tell my family about my incredible sighting. It was almost as if I began rehearsing the story in my head. Something came alive in me when I thought about sharing with those I love as the adventure would be relived by rehearsing the experience. This is our design from God. We're designed to be connected, in good times and in bad.

The story didn't end there. As we returned to the snorkeling area, we were about thirty feet below the surface, and I had no idea we had returned to the boat. I was still glancing over my shoulder nervously hoping to live to tell the story. Dwayne, my brother-in-law, snorkeling on the surface, spotted us. Not knowing anything about what had happened, he simply decided to play a joke on me. Swimming down to me, he clutched my leg as if it were a shark biting me. Needless to say, I thought my life had ended.

The connectivity of our lives is so profound that a variety of studies have been done, revealing this component of our design. A team of researchers at Ohio State University conducted a study inflicting blisters on a test group of married couples. Wounds of hostile couples healed at a rate of 60 percent compared to couples that had low levels of hostility. This research shows that having a happy marriage cuts recovery time from injury and illness almost in half![7]

We are created to be connected. It's fascinating to see in Genesis where God created and said repeatedly, "It is good." Of course, it is good! It's a place of sinless paradise which God himself created for mankind. Before sin ever entered the world, however, God declared something was "not good." Even in the perfect atmosphere of sinless paradise, it is not good that man should be alone because we are created in the image of community God.

As a Trinity, God is a community of Father, Son, and Holy Spirit. This is a community of love, affection, communication, and respect. Every great relationship is enriched with love, affection, communication, and respect. It's the servant nature of God that enriches our lives. True friendship seeks to serve rather than being served. If we rely on other people for appreciation, we end up using them rather than loving them.

When we understand the value of healthy relationships, we begin investing in and valuing people rather than things. The common attitude is to love things and use people. We must work at reversing this for many reasons. Our deepest sense of purpose is born from learning to be part of other people's need.

---

[7]   http://www.cnn.com/2010/HEALTH/06/10/difficult.marriage.health/

Selfishness produces barrenness while selflessness enriches everything it touches. A life of service to Jesus is a life that looks a lot like his purposing inconvenience for the sake of others. It's in this place of purposed inconvenience where we discover purposeful living.

Our children won't learn generosity from their buddies. They must learn it from watching us devote ourselves to loving, serving, and giving so other people's lives are enriched. Our lives are utterly enriched as a result, and legacy becomes our reward.

We are created for this community. Community is about connection, and surface exchanges are not good indicators of true community. True community comes when we are willing to get involved in each other's lives on a deeper level with love as the motivation.

A few years ago, my wife and I watched a documentary where a man ate at McDonalds for every meal over the course of a month. In the course of that time, he gained twenty-four pounds and his liver started shutting down. It was then I realized that in our rushed culture, we can have access to food yet suffer from malnutrition. In a very similar way in our rushed culture, we can have access to people and suffer from relational malnutrition.

In a world that is over-committed and under-connected, we must beware of the barrenness of a busy life.

Rom 12:10 reads, "Be devoted to one another in brotherly love. Honor one another above yourselves" (NIV).

"Brotherly love" speaks of an enriched family love, specifically the love of brothers and sisters. The Greek word that translates *honor* is very interesting and is actually spelled "*time*" in the Greek language.

To honor somebody, we must be willing to share the most valuable commodity we have in our lives—our time. To invest the limited commodity of time into the lives of those around you is to communicate a deep sense of priority and purpose for that connection.

Making room and taking time for the relationships God has entrusted to your care are two of the most rewarding discoveries to make in life. This doesn't happen because you hope it happens. This happens because you learn to be intentional about creating wonderful memories.

Tracy and I bought a fire pit to put in our back yard, not knowing this investment of less than fifty dollars would create a wealth of connection. Multiple times our family would go for a walk into some woods near our house to gather sticks and limbs. A few times, I would find myself dragging a small tree home. Getting the family around that flame somehow produced mesmerizing conversation that deepened the sense of friendship in all of our lives.

These kinds of relationship building opportunities are not complicated or difficult. They just require a little focus time to prepare. Sometimes, our family would take walks. Rather than merely going for a walk, we would draft a list of items that became our scavenger hunt, turning the walk into an adventure. Movie watching is converted from mundane to memorable by laying out a blanket, cooking popcorn, holding flashlights under the chin, and creating your own surprises at key moments in the movie.

We had a friend over to watch *Arachnophobia* on one occasion. Having already seen the movie myself, I knew when a particularly frightening surprise was coming. At just the right time, I tossed my fake spider on my friend. I'm not suggesting you do this as his reaction was borderline violent. Fortunately, he didn't hurt himself and our friendship survived my antics, but years later, this has been something we've laughed about.

Life doesn't have to be mundane and boring. So many people live for the weekend while wasting the week! Enjoy every moment of every day by relationally enriching your world! To receive makes us happy, but to give makes us blessed. It is more blessed to give than to receive. The pursuit of happiness is about how I can get others to make me happy. The pursuit of blessedness is about how I can bless others, and this achieves for me what happiness never could.

Prov 11:24 reads, "The world of the generous gets larger and larger while the world of the stingy gets smaller and smaller" (MSG).

To live a relationally enriched life is to enlarge your perspective to consider others. This increases your world greatly and helps take the focus off from yourself. In 2013, our city suffered devastation from an F5 tornado that destroyed homes, schools, and businesses. It was a terrible tragedy, and unfortunately, lives were lost in the storm.

The community came together in an amazing way. Our church was able to distribute several millions of dollars in supplies, food, clothing, and cash to those in need. There seemed to be two categories of people that we worked with. There were those who focused on what was lost, and there were those who focused on what was left. In no way do I want to minimize the suffering that took place in this tragic event. My observation is not whether people suffered, but how they suffered.

There were families that had suffered terrible loss and devastation, yet in the midst of their pain, they purposed to help others. It was fascinating to see the unstoppable attitude of somebody in need caring for the needs of others. Focusing on what is lost produces grief and paralysis. Focusing on what is left produces thankfulness and purpose. This is an enriching perspective on every level of life.

Perhaps you're reading this right now pondering in your own life what's lost and what's left. Pause in this moment and give thanks to God for what's left. Devote yourself to some enrichment effort over the next twenty-four hours to connect deliberately with somebody you love. How can you take what's left and use it for those you love? This is what enriches the lives of people.

A successful career that costs your marriage and your family is an empty shell of success. This can have an impressive external presentation to others yet be painfully barren. The answer, however, isn't found in marriage or family either. Both marriage and family are also painfully barren when the poverty of community exists in these relationships. It's the enriched connection of a deeper, more meaningful relationship that fosters an enriched life.

Song of Solomon 5:16 provides a wonderful definition of a biblical marriage that possesses true community.

SOS 5:16 states, "This is my lover, and this is my friend" (NIV).

Friendship is incredibly important for the marriage and the family. John Gottman, a sociologist and researcher, who predicts divorce after just minutes in an interview with more than a 90 percent success rate, says that men and women want the exact same thing. Men and women are very different, but 70 percent of both men and women say the most important thing is that their spouse to be their nearest and dearest friend.[8]

We live in a culture that neglects friendship, especially when it comes to romantic relationships. Two people meet, and if there is chemistry between them, they bypass all the steps and stages of forming a friendship by moving straight to romantic behaviors. People come to me for help with their marriage, and very commonly, they can tell me how they met. They can tell me how they fell in love and when

---

[8]   John M Gottman and Nan Silver, *The Seven Principles for Making Marriage Work* (New York: Crown, 1999).

they got married. Very few couples can tell me how they formed a friendship.

Many times I've made the three-month challenge to our congregation. Take a minimum of three months to get to know somebody as friends without expressing any kind of romantic relationship behaviors. Don't kiss, hold hands, embrace, or facilitate any kind of romantic relationship until you've spent months forming the friendship.

Matthew 12:34 teaches us what fills the heart will eventually come out of the mouth. This means your tongue is continually delivering the mail embedded in your heart. Too many times people move swiftly into a relationship without taking the time to read the mail that's coming from the heart. Take the time to read the mail. Take the time to form a friendship. Take the time to get to know the person as a friend before you allow any romantic relationship to develop. The romantic relationship will be greatly enriched by friendship, and later, the friendship will be greatly enriched by the romance.

When friendship is modeled in a marriage, the children are impacted, empowered, and enriched.

1/5/10

Hey Sweetie!

You wrote mommy and daddy letters saying how much you loved us. It was soooo sweet! Love you so much. Thank you for letting us know how much you care. We love you that much back – and more!

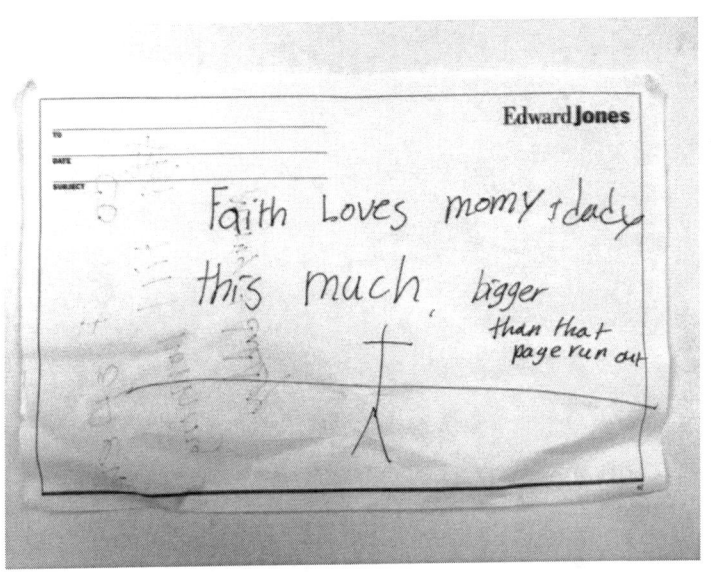

WHAT'S IN YOUR HAND?

JAMES HAD BEEN married for twenty years. Somewhere along the journey, he stopped making meaningful deposits in his marriage. There were tensions and strains along the journey as there are in any relationship, which translate as withdrawals. As is the case in any account, withdrawals without deposits result in bankruptcy. Rather than investing in what was at hand, James began flirting with that which was beyond his reach. One thing led to another, and a damaging relationship erupted. What filled his heart destroyed the treasure in his hand. Tragically, James's marriage ended in divorce, and his children suffered the pain of this unnecessary trauma.

Proper nourishment and concern for the seed in your hand produce a deeper, more meaningful harvest of life. The problem James had is the problem most of us have, the lack of nourishment and concern for the seed will sabotage God's intended harvest. Once today's seed is destroyed, tomorrow's harvest will never be known.

You'd never sell your dreams for any price, but you will exchange them if you're not careful.

Your destiny is discovered in the seed God placed in your hand. How you handle that seed has everything to do with what your life will become. It seems that the enemy is steadily trying to take our focus on what's just beyond our reach. This creates a dangerous disconnection from where we are to where we desire to be. The disconnection produces a willingness to destroy what is in our hand because of the pursuit of what's in our heart.

The seed in a person's hand can completely change a person's life. If the entire world of watermelons as we know it ceased to exist with the exception of just one seed, there would still be hope. That one seed in just one year could produce a watermelon, which, according to *Wiki Answers*, has 300–350 seeds.[9] If we planted three hundred more watermelons the next year, we could have ninety thousand seeds. The following year, we could have nine million seeds.

When God created seed-bearing plants for the first time, it was a miracle. If the plants hadn't had seeds, mankind would have needed miracle after miracle as they ate the plants. Instead, he included mankind in the blessing of

---

9   "How many seeds does the average watermelon have?" (article from *Wiki Answers*)

the seed. We are capable of taking the seed God has provided and multiplying an amazing harvest to impact our future and the future of others if we will discover the blessing of the seed within our reach.

The seed rarely resembles the result. When you look at anything in its seed form, it's difficult if not impossible to determine what it can and will become when treated the way God designed it to be treated. Dreams are seeds. Friendships are seeds. Jobs are seeds.

We have no idea how God is going to bring about life of a supernatural proportion, and figuring this out is not a requirement. We just need to get the one single question right, "What seed has been placed in our hand?" What has God placed within your reach, and how are you faithfully giving yourself to that as the seed that will bring about a harvest?

God never works with what we don't have. He always works with what we do have. When five thousand people had gathered and grew hungry, the disciples wanted to send the people away. Jesus said the people would be fed, and in fact, he told the disciples to feed them. They had to take inventory of what was in their hand. Jesus was fully capable of striking a rock to produce water and perhaps turning the clouds that day into huge loaves of bread that would fall from the sky. Some quail might have also been a nice touch. God was introducing something beyond merely meeting a need. God was revealing the power of understanding that what's in our hand is the key to not only our destiny but also the destiny of countless others as well. The blessing is in the seed.

There is a difference between a blessing and a miracle. When God created trees, it was miraculous. When God caused the seed to grow in the fruit of the trees, it was an invitation to participate in the blessing. The blessing is better than a miracle because it involves us in the process. If the miracle was the extent of how God worked, we'd have to come back over and over asking for more trees to miraculously be created. Instead, God has chosen to involve us in the process of blessing.

The greatest challenge we have in this process is that the seed rarely resembles the harvest. An apple seed doesn't look like an apple, and only through eyes of faith and expectation can we see a tree that can result. Don't grow discouraged by what you don't see in your life. God wants you to be responsible with what's in your hand. In doing so, you are participating in the blessing of God, and a wonderful harvest will result.

Ps 105:17 reads, "He sent a man before them, Joseph, {who} was sold as a slave" (NAS).

God didn't need a slave in Egypt. God needed an influencer, but God's always looking for a starting point. The seed of Joseph's assignment was slavery in Egypt. Joseph was in the right place but had not yet come into the right season to fulfill his assignment. There are reasons for seasons and seasons for reasons. Don't be discouraged by the season of the seed. God has great things in store.

We don't need a great big miracle. We just need a seed!

Your greatest challenge is not between who you are and who you used to be. Your greatest challenge is between who you are and who you're going to be.

God has wonderful plans for our lives. With these plans in mind, he purposes seeds of destiny. What's in your hand is always the key to what God has deposited in your heart. What relationships are in your hand today that need your devoted attention?

When we give our time and energy to more effectively cultivate the seed of relationships entrusted to our care, it unlocks new dimensions of life. One day, I was rushing from one end of the house to the other. As I dashed through the living room, I saw my youngest daughter perplexed by computer woes. Her computer wouldn't work, and she wanted to play games on it that day.

As I blazed by, she verbally reached out to me saying, "Daddy, my computer isn't working." This was more than a passing comment; it was a request for help. I continued my pace, lobbing an excuse in her direction that I was on a deadline for a big project. As I walked out of the room, I immediately realized I just missed an important essay question on the test of life.

After feeble attempts to justify my behavior, I put everything aside and made my way back into the living room, finding the vacant seat on the couch next to my twelve-year-old daughter. Her face went from discouraged to hopeful as she realized I'd come back to offer my help. I'm not a computer wizard, but you would have thought that the smartest computer analyst in the world had come to her rescue.

After less than ten minutes of pecking, powering down, and rebooting, Lexi's computer was up and running again. Rather than just reaching for the computer to play her game, she put her working computer aside and squeezed my arm with sincere appreciation. "Thank you, Daddy!" felt like the equivalent of a million-dollar check that day. Suddenly, I realized that the seed of relationship had been sown. Many families suffer from undue pain and disconnection simply because they neglect what's right within their reach.

The kingdom of God comes with its own set of principles. This is why the rich man had a difficult time and walked away from Jesus. If it were just making him more successful according to the world's successful principles, this successful man would have completely related.

Kingdom principles are seed principles of submission and surrender. To live we must die. To be strong we must become weak. Jesus never demonstrated mastering the world's successful principles as his goal. Jesus ushered in completely new principles attached to eternal values. The kingdom of God is at hand! Life's greatest treasures are within your reach! There is a cross involved, and sacrifice is part of the deal. There could be no resurrection if there had been no crucifixion.

Instead of looking beyond what is in your hand hoping for resurrection pleasure without crucifixion pain, submit completely to that which is within your reach. You'll be amazed at what God can do with what you allow him to work with. So the question is "What's in your hand?"

Jesus came declaring the kingdom is at hand, and all you need is within your reach. The fall of mankind immediately connected the mind of man with temporal limitations as a result of being disconnected from God's eternal perspective. Then Jesus came, introducing the connection to God's kingdom and restoring mankind to this eternal perspective.

With God involved, a little bit is enough to completely renew it all. God's not interested in what you don't have. He wants to bless what you do have. Stop looking at what you don't have, and start giving your very best to what you do have. The blessing is in the seed!

10/27/08

I took you girls for a sunset walk last week. Standing on this hill the sun was setting behind you and it was an incredible sight.

When we all took off running down the hill Faith took a tumble and landed flat. I couldn't help but laugh and it disarmed her concern immediately so she got up laughing, then Lexi started laughing. We laughed all the way home!

Life is wonderful when we make the time to appreciate valuable moments? Life is painful when we miss them.

BOUNDARIES

IN A WORLD that tends to be addicted to rights and blind to obligations, it's easy to miss the joy of celebrating boundaries and discipline. A deeper, more meaningful life is discovered within the boundaries. At first, this seems completely contrary to everything we've been taught about being free. Largely, we don't understand because the world's ideas have evangelized us and converted our thinking in many ways.

School was in session, and the children were playing freely on the playground. Cars were passing by on the busy street, and some of the children were standing at the fence. Fingers clasped through chain link fence, each child had selected the perfect nose-high opening to press their faces against the fence to watch the traffic. One day, there was a discussion about the confinement and limitation that the children were suffering with the restriction of a fence surrounding them like prisoners.

Parents attended school board meetings to voice their concerns and demand the rights for freedom for their children. Emotions were high and the agenda prevailed. Finally, the children were set free and the fence came down. Immediately following, the teachers required all students to stay within fifteen feet of the building as staff diligently tried to stand between the children and the busy street. It was a great distance to the street, but without the fence, dangers were great and freedom was lost.

Jude 1:21 says, "Stay always within the boundaries where God's love can reach and bless you" (TLB).

My two daughters were ages five and six. After school, I picked them up and got them situated in their seatbelts and then announced that we had something to do before going home that day. That next week, I was speaking on this very topic. As we drove home, we met our video team on a busy bridge downtown. I pulled over safely on the side of the road to the right of the line on the shoulder telling the girls, "Wait here and I'll be right back."

Faith and Lexi watched intently as I got out of the car with other cars and semis whisking by at sixty miles per hour rocking the car at times. Standing on the bridge, I faced the camera talking about the rails on the bridge and the lines on the road that provide total freedom for cars to drive within a few feet of each other traveling at high rates of speed.

When we finished the brief shoot, I got back into the car and my girls' eyes were wide open. My oldest daughter exclaimed, "Daddy! Never do that again!" The experience of exploring boundaries that are normally taken for granted made her extremely nervous and rightfully so.

As long as we are living within the boundaries, they are rarely a thought in our minds. Healthy boundaries produce freedom to live life with greater ease of advancement. Understanding and cooperating with the boundaries in life, relationships, work, etc., are such vital parts of possessing a deeper, more meaningful life.

Providing boundaries and stability in any relationship produces confidence and freedom. This empowers two individuals to become more of what God desires them to be. It's the violation of these boundaries that produces deep insecurity leading to deficiency and ultimately dysfunction. Dysfunction is when we dwell in a constant state of mind that violates life's most basic boundaries. This renders us incapable of a life filled with expectation and hope. Dysfunction confines our dreams.

Sometimes we settle for less not because we can't achieve it but because we feel we don't deserve it. In our fallen state of humanity, we are inclined to identify with dysfunction but we are designed to identify with destiny. Some people in the Bible are namelessly known by their dysfunction. There is "the crippled man," "the woman with issue of blood," "the man with a withered hand," and blind Bartamaeus who did get a name but dysfunction still led the way.

Healthy boundaries produce a healthy atmosphere that breeds healthy attitudes. A weekly boundary of dating my wife communicates both ways in our relationship that we are a true priority in each other's lives. The atmosphere of our lives is in constant need of loving deposits to conquer insufficient attitudes that can ultimately leave us with bankrupt lives.

The natural order of our fallen world is for things to simply fall apart. Houses depreciate, cars begin to rust and deteriorate, and if energy and attention aren't devoted to these entities, they completely lose their value. Marriages, friendships, and relationships in general have the same pattern. Unless energy and attention are deposited, the relationship slowly winds down and falls apart. This is why boundaries are so important to consistently strengthen that which we prioritize in our lives.

Randy and Salvador were in high school. Randy was a big football player, and Salvador was an exchange student from Mexico. Salvador slipped back to the bathroom to brush his teeth, and suddenly, he began screaming, "Oh! Oh! Bad! Bad! Very bad!!!" Randy and I ran to the back of the house to see what was going on. Salvador was standing over the toilet spitting profusely trying to get the terrible taste out of his mouth. Thinking he was grabbing the toothpaste, he brushed his teeth with Randy's jock itch cream. I'm not sure what that would be like but I'll take Salvador's word for it, "Bad! Bad! Very Bad!"

Had Salvador taken the time to read the instructions and ask questions if he didn't understand, he would have been spared with that terrible experience. In the same way, if we will take the time to read the Word and ask questions if we don't understand biblical boundaries, we can be spared much heartache. Great blessing is discovered in the boundaries where God can protect us. Great anguish can result when we violate those boundaries and move beyond his protective reach. This can be bad, bad, very bad.

The Bible is full of boundaries, and they are not restrictions and limitations as much as they are protectors and liberators.

Ex 23:19 reads, "Do not cook a young goat in its mother's milk" (NIV).

Scientifically, we now understand that cooking a goat in milk causes the bacteria of the milk to absorb into the meat. Drinking milk is no problem because liquid processes through our bodies quickly enough so the bacteria have no effect. When the bacteria remain as a result of the slower process of meat digestion, there is a problem. The bacteria in the meat putrefy and can poison the blood stream. This boundary wasn't to restrict but rather to protect.

Lev 12:3 states, "On the eighth day the boy is to be circumcised" (NIV).

Leviticus reveals that a baby is to wait until the eighth day after being born before being circumcised. When a baby is born, there is a process of adapting from the disconnection of the mother's immune system to developing its own. Interestingly enough, this process takes about a week. With sterile conditions today, this is no longer a medical concern, but obviously, this was a protective boundary in these days of the Bible, allowing the child's immune system to be in place before the procedure.

The Bible speaks repeatedly about relational boundaries of loving, serving, and giving. When we apply these principles selflessly, our relationships flourish. There is nothing more wonderful than two selfless people in a relationship working to stay within these biblical boundaries together. There is nothing more painful than two selfish people in a relationship violating these biblical boundaries.

After twenty-four years of marriage, my wife and I have a very good understanding of what it takes to encourage and strengthen each other. Knowing the information and applying it to the relationship are two different things. I'm a pretty romantic guy. The truth is I'm not very good at it but I try. Tracy appreciates my efforts though many times they don't work out the way I wish they would.

One evening, I envisioned a night under the stars with my wife. My hope was that we would lie there in the night looking up and maybe even seeing a shooting star before the night was over. The biggest problem was that we lived in a metro area of a million people and seeing the stars with the city lights wasn't easy. I actually laid out a blanket on the rooftop of our house. When Tracy arrived home, I took her by the hand and led her to the ladder in the back yard propped against the house. The night was clear and the stars were amazing. The problem is that the pitch of the roof was so steep she kept sliding down as I was trying to hold her up.

My romantic efforts continue even though my blunders have been many. In one instance, I was speaking at a conference. Chairs had been moved around during an enthusiastic time of worship, and as I got the nod that I was about to be called up, I reached over and gave an affirming pat to my wife's behind. As I started walking to the platform, I noticed my wife was actually standing in front of me. The lady beside me that I'd just affirmed inappropriately was not my wife! Immediately, I went to one of the leaders explaining the mistake before speaking in case a complaint was filed before I could come down from the platform to defend myself.

Certain expressions in my marriage relationship communicate a romantic inclination shared by two lovers. This area of our lives is clearly an area of boundaries that should never be shared with others. That night as I accidentally stepped out of those boundaries, I was embarrassed and humiliated. After I spoke, I actually went to the woman and her husband with my wife by my side explaining and apologizing. The woman never even knew it had taken place and assumed somebody had brushed against her.

The reality exists that when certain boundaries are crossed, life suddenly changes. Once you've moved beyond the boundaries, you may think you're in control, but you're really not. You can drive seventy miles per hour in a twenty-five-miles-per-hour zone while it's raining and not be skidding at first. This can deceive you into feeling like you're in control, but it won't be long until the painful reality of just how out of control you truly are sets in.

Life is best when it's lived within the proper boundaries that sustain freedom and produce life. Take the time. Make the time. Don't be deceived into thinking you can live beyond the boundaries and be fine. Invest in relationships on a routine basis showing your love for those who mean so much in your life. This is the key to deeper, more meaningful relationships. This is the key to a deeper, more meaningful life.

BOUNDARIES: 6-26-04

Dear Lexi,

Today you and I spent about 3 hours in the emergency room at the Children's Hospital. Since I'd just returned from a trip I wanted to spend some extra time with you and Faith. We'd gone to McDonalds and you guys had played having a wonderful time. On the way home Faith asked if I'd put the top down on the car. I pulled over and pushed the button. I said my usual phrase, "Fingertips on noses" to protect your little limbs from the metal contraption as it folded the top down over your heads.

You removed your finger and lifted your arm into the metal bars as it was retracting and it took your arm with it. I was horrified when I realized what happened and I couldn't get your arm out at first. Finally I got you free. Faith was screaming at me telling me I was hurting you. You were screaming and crying in terrific pain.

Fortunately there were no broken bones. The emergency room doctor said she was certain it wasn't broken. Possible slight fracture but she doubted it so she just sent us on our way.

Love you so much. When you hurt I hurt. Can't stand to see my girls in pain. I went out with mommy tonight on a date and you were all I could think about the entire time. We came home early so I could kiss you and tuck you in. night night...

LISTEN WELL

WHEN WE NEGLECT listening, we are left to live within the prison of our own limitations. You'll never know what you need until you know what you're not. People who don't take the time to listen to the voices of people around them will eventually find themselves surrounded by people who have nothing to say.

We are born with the ability to hear, but we must learn the skill of listening. Listening is the single most valuable skill in communication. We dignify others when we take the time to listen to what they have to say. This requires us to learn how to care about the person behind the words. This is not about a mere exchange of words. Conversation, communication, and listening are the avenues through which a relationship transforms people into what the relationship is capable of helping them become.

Of course, our proportionate design speaks clearly of our need to listen twice as much as we speak. It is interesting that *listen* and *silent* are spelled with the same letters. As long as your total focus is communicating your views and opinions, you'll never discover the greater potential of the wonderful relationships that have been entrusted to your care.

A young man worked eagerly to make an appointment with a very important man, hoping to glean wisdom about decisions he needed to make for his future. After weeks, he was given a thirty-minute appointment. Nervously, he sat in the waiting room when finally the thirty minutes began. "Mr. Gascoyne will see you now." The young man entered the large office aware of the very busy schedule this important leader kept. He explained he'd come hoping for input and wisdom. To his surprise, Mr. Gascoyne removed his watch and turned it upside down on the desk. This small expression of availability communicated very clearly that Mr. Gascoyne was interested in listening and not rushing through an appointment.

Many times in our relationships, the signals we send communicate that we are distracted from a deeper, more meaningful conversation. When our eyes are focused in another direction or our brain is racing in other places, we are not listening. Learning the art of communicating that mentally we've taken off our watch and turned it upside down on the desk makes for a meaningful and enriching exchange. This should be our goal in every conversation opportunity with those we love.

The way you listen communicates how much you value the conversation. If you've already made up your mind, then conversation coming your way is seen as a threat that can confuse your conclusions. If you've determined that your position is supreme, then you're only listening long enough to make an assessment so you can give advice. Some people have determined that asking questions is the best way to communicate, yet this doesn't ensure that good communication is taking place.

The key to great listening is to look beyond the words and capture the heart behind what is being spoken. This is where you peel back the words to see the deeper meaning of conversation and its origin in the other person's life. Nonverbal communication such as facial expression, body language, and tone is a contributor to what's truly being said. Life's experiences, both good and bad, come through with potential to express years of wisdom when we get to deeper, more meaningful places of conversational exchange. A great listener looks for the substance behind the words because he or she is genuinely interested in seeing a bigger picture. I'll repeat the opening statement of this chapter, "When we neglect listening we are left to live within the prison of our own limitations."

The Bible speaks of the value of listening and gathering wisdom. I've learned in life that we learn God's truths by instruction or we can learn by correction. The easy way to learn is to gather information and avoid mistakes in advance. Learning the hard way results when we choose not to listen and have to make the mistakes on our own before we learn from them.

Prov 21:11 reads, "Simpletons only learn the hard way, but the wise learn by listening" (The Message).

Talking too much lessens our ability to listen and learn. In addition, it's a terrible habit in general. Mark Twain said, "Noise proves nothing. Often a hen who has merely laid an egg cackles as if she had just laid an asteroid." Talk is cheap in our world because supply exceeds demand. Abraham Lincoln said, "He can compress the most words into the smallest ideas of any man I ever met." An abundance of words can be an indication that a cover up is taking place.

Matt 25:14-15 says, "Again, it will be like a man going on a journey, who called his servants and entrusted his property to them. To one he gave five talents of money, to another two talents, and to another one talent, each according to his ability. Then he went on his journey" (NIV).

It's interesting to me that reading on in this passage reveals that the first two servants doubled their investments and said so in just thirteen words. However, the third servant, who accomplished nothing, gave his report with more than three times the amount of explanation using forty-three words.

When your conscience is at ease, you don't feel the need to explain. As a school principal years ago, I can easily recall the nervous chatter that would erupt from students when they knew they'd been caught doing something they shouldn't. Distractions, blame shifting, and explanations would bubble out like a spewing bottle of root beer.

Jesus, the man who knew everything, lived a life on the earth that was marked by asking questions. Genuinely pursuing a greater understanding of the people around us is very glorifying to God, dignifying to people and honoring to relationships. To listen well, we must work at listening without an agenda. Deeper, more meaningful relationships result from serving, loving, and giving selflessly into the lives of those we care about so much.

Relational substance is only discovered through intentional connection. Jesus was walking through a crowd of people; Luke 8:42 states, "the crowds almost crushed him" (NIV). The crowd of people was crushing around him trying to see this Jesus that so many were talking about. Interestingly enough, Jesus asks this incredible question identifying the intentional touch of one person in an entire crowd that was crowded and bumping against him. Mark 5:30–31 says, "He turned around in the crowd and asked, 'Who touched my clothes?' 'You see the people crowding against you,' his disciples answered, 'and yet you can ask, "Who touched me?"'" (NIV).

The disciples were astonished at such a question. Masses of people were bumping up against Jesus, yet he took note that somebody was intentional about their touch as he asked, "Who touched me?" In our lives, it's very easy to go about our devotions, reading quick prayers over meals and brief expressions of prayer in God's direction merely brushing against him and bumping him. Jesus takes note when somebody is intentional about reaching out to touch him.

God doesn't just want your attention. He wants your affection. You can give God your attention without offering your affection, and this results in a relational deficiency. Any relationship in your life that possesses mere attention with no affection is a relationship that lacks substance. Both are vital to a deeper, more meaningful relationship, and this requires being intentional about connecting, listening, and growing deeper together.

The power of conversation is greater than we realize. When God introduced himself personally to our world, he introduced himself as "The Word." Obviously, he's a very conversational God! Prayer isn't committing to say certain things before God. Prayer is conversation with God drawing near to his heart so we can listen well to our Creator.

Ex 33:11 reads, "The LORD would speak to Moses face to face, as a man speaks with his friend" (NIV).

Is this possible for us? Many Christians have decided not to let the Bible get in the way of what they want to believe. The Bible clearly tells us how intimate conversation is God's plan for relationship with mankind.

John 10:27 states, "My sheep listen to my voice; I know them, and they follow me" (NIV).

Isa 30:21 reads, "Your ears will hear a word behind you, 'This is the way, walk in it,' whenever you turn to the right or to the left" (NAS).

There was a massive tsunami on December 26, 2004. It was triggered by a magnitude 9 Indian Ocean earthquake, killing more than 150,000 people in a dozen countries.[10]

National Geographic recently did a report stating that just before this catastrophic event took place, elephants screamed and ran for higher ground. Dogs refused to go outdoors. Flamingos abandoned their low-lying breeding areas. Regardless of your explanation, the reality exists that there is more to our world than meets the eye. [11]

Multiple times my daughter has written in her journal exact phrases and verses that various speakers and ministers speak the day after she's written them down. I've witnessed this as she has explained it to me on various occasions after the speaker speaks and then she shows me her journal that night when we would arrive home.

---

[10] "2004 Indian Ocean earthquake and tsunami" (article from *Wikipedia*)

[11] http://news.nationalgeographic.com/news/2004/12/ 1227_041226_tsunami.html

Ben and Holly were believing for a baby. As I began praying for them, I sensed the Holy Spirit speaking to me that they would have twins. I shared this word, and in time, Blake and Kinley were born together fulfilling that word.

Recently, I stopped in and surprised a ministry team in Plano, TX. A young man who was part of that team was astonished when he saw me standing there. It had been months since I'd last ministered in that church, yet he explained how he felt the Holy Spirit was bringing my name to his attention several times that particular day. There is more going on than we care to admit, and it's a mistake to pretend we understand it completely. God is constantly making announcements, and we must prepare our hearts to listen well when he speaks.

Isa 42:9 says, "See, the former things have taken place, new things I declare; before they spring into being I announce them to you" (NIV).

The Scripture says God makes these announcements. We're all guilty of going numb when announcements start coming our way. *CBS News* reports that the average American experiences as many as five thousand advertisements, or announcements, every day. It's very easy to become numb to the announcements in our culture. Certainly, this is the case with God's announcements. We are so distracted or entertained that we can't even hear his voice. When I was a boy, I would be so engrossed in a movie that my parents struggled to get my attention. Now, my children do the same thing. Perhaps this has been an issue with God and his children throughout the ages!

It's important that we cultivate a personal atmosphere that fosters conversation with God. Atmosphere really does serve a major role in every area of our lives. The right atmosphere sets the tone for romance on a date. The right atmosphere can set the tone for open and vulnerable conversation with our children. The right atmosphere sets the tone for fruitful conversation with God. Wake up in the morning a little early this week every day and create an atmosphere of conversation with God. Brew your coffee, light a candle, turn some worship music on, read your Bible, and purpose intimate moments with God. You'll be amazed at how this will initiate a conversation with God that will continue throughout your day!

Our church congregation specifically focused on this for a season of time. Everybody made an extra effort to purpose to listen well. To encourage each other to find these places, we all committed to take a picture of the prayer spot and post it online with a hashtag "#PrayAttention." Pictures ranged from beautiful scenery to back yard furniture including candles, Bibles, and authentic expressions of atmosphere.

Prov 8:34 reads, "Blessed is the man or woman who listens to me, awake and ready for me each morning" (The Message).

This lifestyle of listening well to God is greatly enhanced by an annual focus I've promoted for years during the time many people are making New Year's resolutions. Instead of merely focusing on areas of our lives we desire to improve, we should discover the things God has in mind for our new year. New Year's resolutions are great, but New Year's revelations are better. Each year, the focus is to discover a specific word, phrase, or scripture that will be my thematic focus for the year from God.

Over the years, this has been a tremendous help for me to learn how to listen well. When I find myself stuck in a rut trying to figure out how to keep my quiet time fresh, I simply return to my New Year's revelation for that year and explore it deeper. This has brought amazing purpose to my pursuit of God.

One year, the Lord spoke to me that it was to be a year of "rocks, remember, and review." At first, I was at a total loss, so I began studying the Bible looking for rocks. I quickly found where the Israelites would experience God's miraculous intervention in their lives. They would pile rocks to later rehearse when passing that way with the next generation. I had my entire focus that year as I discovered this.

Tracy and I spent twelve months focusing on the meaningful places in our marriage. We took our daughters back to the place where we met. We took them to the place where we first kissed. We took great delight in grossing them out by kissing each other standing in that spot right on the mouth! I spent many hours traveling back to my roots thanking God for his faithfulness in my life and the many experiences I'd simply neglected to rehearse. It was an enriching year in my relationship with Jesus, and it all came from simply listening well.

Listening well to God produces a deeper, more meaningful purpose in all of our relationships. Discovering God's purposes for every connection that exists in our lives is enriching, rewarding, and enlightening. This is a deeper, more meaningful life.

8/9/10

Dear Tracy,

It's really true that words simply cannot express how privileged I feel to be sharing life with you. You're a wonderful wife, partner, parent, lawyer, etc, etc, etc.

I'm so thankful for your influence in my life and in our girls' lives. They both received the Christian Testimony awards at school! Last week, I was thanking the girls for being so obedient to us on every occasion. Faith looked at me and said, "Wow dad I'm going to live a long time huh?" Apparently you'd had a conversation recently about honoring your father and mother and it will go well with you all the days of your life. As I responded affirming her conclusion she then responded, "Uh oh dad… Gavin may not live very long because he's very disobedient."

I thought I was going to wreck the car I was laughing so hard. Then we prayed for Gavin.

CONCLUSION

HOPE IS NOT A STRATEGY

THE CONCLUSION OF this book has come and the next chapter of a deeper, more meaningful life is up to you. Don't just hope for a deeper, more meaningful life. Hope is not a strategy and hope alone won't be enough. Inspiration without application breeds frustration.

Knowing what we need to do is one thing. Doing what we know to do is another. Make a list of five people who you would consider to be meaningful relationships in your life. Start devoting time, energy and money to invest in these relationships with the purpose of enriching the lives of these people you care about.

As a former teacher I figured out over time that my class productivity was much higher if I took the time to greet my students at the door as they came into the classroom. Offering a smile and a greeting seemed to make a deposit in the students that was quickly returned as the bell would ring and class would begin. Basic kindness and consideration are part of God's design for our lives.

Bringing sunshine into somebody else's life automatically produces it in your own. You can't demand heat from a fire if you've not provided wood. You can't demand interest from a bank if you've not made an investment. Our lives are like sponges and once saturated we can't absorb more until we are squeezed out. Making the most of your life doesn't help others. However, helping others does make the most of your life.

Eph 2:10 says, "It is God himself who has made us what we are and given us new lives from Christ Jesus; and long ages ago he planned that we should spend these lives in helping others" (TLB).

Abraham understood that the reason he was blessed was so he could be a blessing. In blessing others you end up rewarding yourself. One thing always leads to another. Before you realize it deeper, more meaningful patterns will materialize in your life and the lives of those you care about.

You will never leave a legacy until you first live a legacy. Get started as soon as you put this book down.

BIBLIOGRAPHY

The Grass Grows on Your Path. *Today in the Word*, June 29, 1992.

Bombeck, Erma. *Forever, Erma: best-loved writing from America's favorite humorist*. Kansas City: Andrews and McMeel, 1996.

Batson, C. Daniel. ""From Jerusalem To Jericho": A Study Of Situational And Dispositional Variables In Helping Behavior." *Journal of Personality and Social Psychology*: 100-108. (accessed June 28, 2013).

Bits & Pieces, June 23, 1994.

Parrish, R. Gibson. "Profile of Mortality from the 1989 Loma Prieta Earthquake using Coroner and Medical Examiner Reports." *Disasters*: 160-170. (accessed July

20, 2013). 2010. Haiti quake death toll rises to 230,000. *BBC*, February 10.

Cohen, Elizabeth, and Sabriya Rice. "Is your marriage making you sick?" CNN. http://www.cnn.com/2010/HEALTH/06/10/difficult.marriage.health/ (accessed July 13, 2013).

Gottman, John Mordechai, and Nan Silver. *The seven principles for making marriage work*. New York: Crown Publishers, 1999.

Answers Corporation. "How many seeds does the average watermelon have?" WikiAnswers. http://wiki.answers.com/Q/How_many_seeds_does_the_average_watermelon_have (accessed July 20, 2013).

Wikimedia Foundation. "2004 Indian Ocean earthquake and tsunami." Wikipedia. http://en.wikipedia.org/wiki/2004_Indian_Ocean_earthquake_and_tsunami (accessed July 28, 2013).

National Geographic Society. "The Deadliest Tsunami in History?" National Geographic. http://news.nationalgeographic.com/news/2004/12/1227_041226_tsunami.html (accessed July 28, 2013).